IT'S TIME TO EAT GRAPE SALAD

It's Time to Eat GRAPE SALAD

Walter the Educator

Silent King Books
A WhichHead Entertainment Imprint

Copyright © 2024 by Walter the Educator

All rights reserved. No part of this book may be reproduced in any manner whatsoever without written per- mission except in the case of brief quotations embodied in critical articles and reviews.

First Printing, 2024

Disclaimer

This book is a literary work; the story is not about specific persons, locations, situations, and/or circumstances unless mentioned in a historical context. Any resemblance to real persons, locations, situations, and/or circumstances is coincidental. This book is for entertainment and informational purposes only. The author and publisher offer this information without warranties expressed or implied. No matter the grounds, neither the author nor the publisher will be accountable for any losses, injuries, or other damages caused by the reader's use of this book. The use of this book acknowledges an understanding and acceptance of this disclaimer.

It's Time to Eat GRAPE SALAD is a collectible early learning book by Walter the Educator suitable for all ages belonging to Walter the Educator's Time to Eat Book Series. Collect more books at WaltertheEducator.com

USE THE EXTRA SPACE TO TAKE NOTES AND DOCUMENT YOUR MEMORIES

GRAPE SALAD

It's time to eat, hooray, hooray!

It's Time to Eat

Grape Salad

A yummy treat is on the way.

Round and juicy, red and green,

Grapes so shiny, fresh, and clean!

We pluck them off the little vine,

Each one sweet, a snack divine.

Crunchy walnuts join the fun,

This grape salad's number one!

A creamy swirl, a drizzle bright,

Honey or yogurt, just a light bite.

Mix it gently, don't rush through,

It's looking yummy, so are you!

Little hands can help prepare,

Tossing grapes with loving care.

Big or small, we're all a team,

Making salads feels like a dream.

It's Time to Eat

Grape Salad

We sit together, fork in hand,

This treat is better than we planned.

Crunch and munch, we laugh, we cheer,

Grape salad brings us all so near.

What's your favorite, green or red?

Both are tasty, it must be said!

Every bite is sweet and cool,

Grape salad makes us all drool!

One last bite, then maybe more,

This salad's something we adore.

Healthy, fresh, and oh so neat,

Grape salad is the best to eat!

Now the bowl is empty, oh no!

But don't be sad, we'll make more, you know.

Let's clean up and start anew,

It's Time to Eat

Grape Salad

Grape salad fun for me and you!

Grapes are magic, don't you see?

They grow on vines and climb with glee.

From nature's hand to our own plate,

Grape salad truly is first-rate!

So every time it's snack time here,

Let's make grape salad with a cheer.

It's tasty, healthy, fun to make,

It's Time to Eat

Grape Salad

The perfect treat we all can take!

ABOUT THE CREATOR

Walter the Educator is one of the pseudonyms for Walter Anderson. Formally educated in Chemistry, Business, and Education, he is an educator, an author, a diverse entrepreneur, and he is the son of a disabled war veteran. "Walter the Educator" shares his time between educating and creating. He holds interests and owns several creative projects that entertain, enlighten, enhance, and educate, hoping to inspire and motivate you. Follow, find new works, and stay up to date with Walter the Educator™ at WaltertheEducator.com

www.ingramcontent.com/pod-product-compliance
Lightning Source LLC
LaVergne TN
LVHW052012060526
838201LV00059B/3991